Adding Quality To Life

*Living Your Best Life In Spite
Of Your Circumstances*

Ryan M. McLean

BALBOA.PRESS
A DIVISION OF HAY HOUSE

Balboa Press books may be ordered through booksellers or by contacting:

Balboa Press
A Division of Hay House
1663 Liberty Drive
Bloomington, IN 47403
www.balboapress.com
844-682-1282

Print information available on the last page.

ISBN: 979-8-7652-3863-9 (sc)
ISBN: 979-8-7652-3864-6 (e)

Balboa Press rev. date: 02/16/2023

Contents

Preface

History

There was a time when I believed that fitness and nutrition were two abstract subjects to be studied in a classroom and were unrelated to our daily lives.

Later in life I realized that fitness and nutrition has affected my life since as early as I can remember. Like many families, we often communicated our love and affection for one another through food. Needless to say, in my household there was an abundance of love and "food". The eating occasions varied from fast food on family road trips, celebrations, holidays, and any other communal occasion you can imagine.

To deny my brother and me food, my mother felt, was the equivalent of denying us love. I believe my brother and I learned that early on and boy did we take advantage of it. I can say specifically for myself, that I gained the most amount of weight from the age of 10 to 13. I now recognize what caused the sudden boom in weight gain during those years. Ruben and I (Ruben being two and a half years older) had finally reached the age where we could be trusted to stay home by ourselves after school. The earlier years were spent at the homes of trusted friends and family. In those times, we ate things like Ramen noodles and pork and beans after school. But now with this new frontier of "fending" for ourselves, our poor mother would be bombarded with desperate cries of starvation on her way home from work. I'll give it to her, she put up some resistance in the beginning, exclaiming that there was plenty of food in the house or to wait until she got home because she had plans to cook. But we would hear none of it, and eventually she caved like a diligent mother bird to the persistent squalls of her chicks. Monday through Friday it became routine that we ate at a variety of fast-food spots. Burger King, Mc Donald's, Taco Bell, Wendy's, and often Ruben would request one place and I another. During those years we were like partners in crime, when he ate, I ate, and we had gotten big together. Although we shared similar eating habits, our personalities are drastically different. Where I loved to rip and run and socialize, Ruben preferred to stay to himself. We suffered our fair share of bullying.

It was hard on both of us, but we chose to deal with it differently. Ruben would isolate himself and turn to food for comfort, where my desire for acceptance would not allow me to retreat. I didn't play sports and would mainly just hang around while the other kids in the neighborhood did. The older I got (around the age of 13) the more adventurous I became. This was a time when I had a lot more freedom to travel beyond the limits of my neighborhood. Equipped with a bike, I found myself in the house a lot less and the streets a lot more. Naturally my partnership with Ruben came to an end, and he was left to order food for himself while I ran the streets until the streetlights came on. Unbeknownst to me, the weight began to fall off and I simultaneously experienced a growth spurt. Now at the age of 14 I found myself entering high school with a new image and an elevated self-esteem. Although this newfound image was not so closely associated with food, it was now replaced with the things of the streets. I began to indulge in cigarettes, as well as drugs and alcohol. I traded in one destructive lifestyle for another. At the age of 15 I found myself in a juvenile detention center. There, I believe was the first time I was exposed to weightlifting by a professional.

Everyone called him coach. He was the staff member assigned to the gym. I played football (badly) my freshmen year of high school, so the concept of exercise was not foreign to me. Yet it was something about the gym setting with a trainer that stuck with me. Quite possibly it was the "personal" aspect of the training that had such an impact. After spending a month in Juvy and my charge subsequently dropped, I returned home with a new vigor about me. In part, of course, because being locked up added to this bad boy image I was cultivating, but also the absence of drugs and alcohol coupled with the exercise routines I was learning had inspired me. Once on the streets again, it was business as usual, and I was back to my old tricks. Hanging with the same friends and getting high. There was a new twist though. I began to implore my friends to lift weights with me on the universal weight set my father put in our basement years ago that we never used. I also would ask my friend "Ready" to give us access to the gym in his apartment complex so we could work out. Most common were the days after a long night of partying; I would go to the park and try to run some of the toxins out of my system. During those times, I "straddled the fence" heavily teetering back and forth between fitness and foolishness. Ultimately, I could not maintain the balancing act. The field you sow seeds in is where you will bear fruit. For many like myself, we never fully make decision as to what it is we want out life and what direction we should be headed. This inconsistency of purpose will disrupt progress every time.

By the age of 17 shortly before my 18th birthday, the energy invested in the streets finally paid dividends, landing me in the county jail, facing life in prison. Scared would be an understatement. This was not juvy and I was not a hardened criminal. In my mind I was flooded with the stereotypical images of prison. Expecting to walk into a gladiator's arena. The reality of the situation was far from what I had imaged. Of course, you had your fair share of violence, but the Spartanesque characters you see on TV is either an exaggeration or the reminiscence of jail in its antiquity and the same holds true for prison. After being forcibly uprooted from what I knew to be normal, I now sat in the county jail, free from the freedom to continue "some" of my destructive behavioral patterns. With the prospect of possibly spending the remainder of my life in prison, I was compelled to reflect upon what lead me up to this point and what direction I wanted to lead in moving forward. All I knew was that I did not want to be here and did not want to associate with the people and things that got me here. They say, "doing the same thing expecting a different result is a form of insanity", and I certainly was not insane. Misguided albeit, but not insane. Jail and prison are just microcosms of society at large. Although everyone has allegedly committed a crime, you will find all types of characters behind the wall. Some nice, some mean, some fat, some lean and everything in between. The stereotypical prisoner simply doesn't exist. Therefore, the question I had to answer is "If you are no longer who you were, who will you be?" That question would eventually fuel my journey on the road to a healthy lifestyle.

During my stay in county, and newly empowered with a trajectory for my life, it was as if the world around me began to change or at least my view of it. The crowds that I once socialized in had lost their appeal, and the things that once held my interest, were now looked upon as mere distractions.

I had begun to form friendships with anyone whom I came across who worked out. We often held each other accountable and motivated one another to remain consistent in our workouts. The most impactful person during my stay in the county jail was a brother named "Streets". He was in his mid-thirties and a mixed martial arts fighter. I had encountered a lot of people that said they used to box or fight professionally, but at looking at them, you couldn't tell that they had ever been involved in any type of physical activity, let alone professionally. Yet, with Streets you could tell. He was into something that turned him into a virtual specimen, and whatever it was, I was eager to find out. I would bombard him with questions which eventually showed him that I had a genuine interest in what it took to get like him.

There is a saying that goes, "they want my glory but don't know my story" and boy is that true! I did not know what I was signing up for when I chose Streets as a mentor. The training he put me through was rigorous as well as non-negotiable. I came to him for guidance so there was no compromise. Like a drill sergeant, he would come to my cell the moment they let us out in the morning, and we would work out for no less than an hour every morning. The workouts were always complex and creative. Seemingly concocted somewhere in the far reaches of his mind. He had the innate ability of utilizing all the limited space and resources around us. Those initial work out experiences have remained with me to this day. The pace and level at which I was working lead me to believe that in the span of a few months, I had shaped my physique to rival his own. How delusional was I? To believe that a former chunky child turned tall, and slinky drug addict could become a fitness model in a matter of a few months was a bit of a stretch. Call me delusional or optimistic, all I know is that I saw progress.

My experience with Streets was just one piece of the puzzle, which would ultimately cultivate the healthy lifestyle I desired to lead. The reality of the progress I had made was made apparent when I sent a picture of myself to one of my lady friends. Expecting praise and words of affirmation for how good I looked, I was surprised and a little hurt when she exclaimed that I looked "so sad." "What do you mean sad!" I shot back. "How could she not recognize all of this work I have put in" was the only thought in my mind. She then proceeded to explain that my face looked gaunt, exaggerating my already pronounced jaw and cheek bones. I couldn't understand how I was putting in all of this work, yet still not achieving my ideal body. A blow to my ego as it was, I did not allow that to discourage me. I continued the hard work well after my conviction and subsequent arrival to prison.

Now prison was an entirely new battlefield. I had the misfortune of being sent to Maryland's Supermax security prison at the age of 19. This new environment consisted of completely new obstacles on top of those I had just recently tackled. Unlike the county jail where everyone for the most part was sober, prison made it a lot easier for someone to slip back into their old habits if they had any. I don't believe you can truly say you're over a thing without having access to it. The test comes in when you have the opportunity to do something, and you chose not to. As for myself, I was not as disciplined as my experience in county had led me to believe. One of my old vices reared its ugly head. You could imagine my surprise when I discovered that dudes knew how to make alcohol. In my mind, it was a momentary escape, an opportunity to reconnect with the past. A past that had alluded me for the year plus that I was in county. But see the thing about dredging up the past is that you only intend to reconnect to the good times, but everything else comes with it. I found myself socializing with similar characters that I had once distanced myself from. Here, drinking buddies were in abundance as well as workout partners, but no real accountability partner. It seemed like almost everyone was straddling the fence when it came to either their health or their habit. Myself included. Luckily, the safeguard I had in place that would prevent me from doing a complete back slide into old habits was the year of hard work and discipline that I was not willing to flush down the toilet. I now lived on the fence. Doing the best balancing act of fitness and foolishness that you could imagine. My thinking was that although alcohol was prohibited in prison, it was often overlooked, and it was legal on the streets. I was never criticized or frowned upon, so no harm no foul right!?!

The years flew by, and I had reached the age of 23. I saw subtle changes in my appearance but not the significant ones that I expected. Feeling stagnated in my growth, I began experimenting with the nutritional side of things. At the time, my diet consisted of the three meals provided by the institution (sometimes with extras) and all the junk I could afford on commissary. The only significant change I made was subtracting roman noodles from my diet. There was an associate of mine that had went on lock up for about a month, and upon his return, during one of our basketball games, he commented that I had gotten a six pack while he was gone. In Hine sight, I can attribute the development to my change of diet, but at the time I was just as amazed as he was. After serious contemplation, I determined that it had to be the noodles because nothing significant had changed in my workout routine for years.

Empowered not only with new but fast results, I began consuming all the fitness advice I could garner. Informally, this was yet another piece of the puzzle. I had a pitch patch job of exercise and nutritional trial and error.

Around the same year (2015) I met a brother named KD. We gravitated towards each other because of our shared interest in working out. But unlike anyone else that I had met during my incarceration, he was the first person to point me in the academic direction of my health and wellness interests. I was given a brochure from Strafford Career Institute where I enrolled and graduated with a diploma in fitness and nutrition as well as natural health consultant. The trajectory of my life had come back into focus. The final piece of the puzzle had arrived, and I could see the bigger picture. I learned about the relationship and reactions our bodies have to the things we put in it, down to a molecular level. Faced with the truth of how alcohol was affecting my body, I decided that drinking was contrary to the things I believe in. It has been amazing how much my Life has changed with the knowledge and implementation of the things I have learned. Fitness and nutrition have taught me that to change one's thinking is to change one's reality. Regardless of one's circumstance, it is always possible to improve your quality of life.

Chapter 1

People, Places, Things

In order to make an effectual change, we are continuously reminded that we must change "people, places, and things". If you haven't heard the saying, I would wager that you are living under a rock. The idea is simply put but often times fails to convey a path to proper execution. The argument has also been made that sometimes these factors are unchangeable. I would have to whole hearty agree in part. Especially as it pertains to one's upbringing. We cannot choose the families we are born into, the communities we are raised, nor the things we are taught in the most formative years of our lives. In these early stages of life, you are at your most impressionable.

Behavioral patterns developed here often follow you the rest of your life. By the time we reach a certain age, some of us have adopted such bad habits, where to present them with an alternative view is to challenge their reality. Other factors that maybe out of our control are that we might be incarcerated, in or live in an impoverished, food desert community. All the previously mentioned are by all means obstacles, but these obstacles are surmountable. Your "life" regardless of where you are in it should have a "style" of your liking. I have seen plenty of people, both on the streets as well as in prison that dress in a manner that is not reflective of any obstacle that has been presented to them. Like the thrifty fashionista, many must get creative when desiring to live a healthy lifestyle. Also, for those with access to the best of resources, you too must be creative when putting them all together. You may still protest in spite of all that I have just said, professing that "you are not influenced by anyone or anything" or that "you once had it all together and you can just as easily get back on track". I commend those who assume responsibility for their lives.

Reading this book alone, shows that you have a desire to do so. Yet, similar to being in court, where it's the state's burden to prove your guilt and once convicted, your burden to win an appeal. We are affected by a litany of societal influences which far too often have self-destructive consequences, subsequently leaving us with the sole burden of cleaning up the mess that our lives have become. Mess can be a difficult word for anyone to ascribe to their life. But let's "call a spade a shovel". Any area in your life where you find inconsistency, disorder, disarray, denial, and depression amongst other things, you should consider that it might be safe to say that there are some messy areas that could use a bit of cleaning. Now, letting this book be your new nose, I think it's time that we try and sniff out some of those messy people in our lives.

People/Relationships

Every relationship has its purpose/purposes. When cleaning up this area of your life, it is imperative that you comb through it with a fine-tooth comb, leaving no stone unturned. Take a good look at your friends and other associates. But there may come a time when you have to look at your wife, husband, mother, father, sister, brother, and maybe even grandma with the side eye. Remember, the burden is on you to create the healthy life that you wish to lead. There has even been language created to exemplify the toxicity of many relationships. The Merriam Webster's Collegiate Dictionary has defined codependency as "a psychological condition or relationship in which a person is controlled or manipulated by another who is affected with a pathological condition (as an addiction to alcohol or heroin)." Many of us have addictions to drugs, alcohol, and/or food which we bring to the relationship table. It is natural to want to share your interests with the ones you care about regardless of how damaging it may be. Some people also will genuinely attempt to improve upon developing relationships by way of things like gift giving, quality time, and giving advice. What may very well be done with the best intent, depending on where the giver is in their own life, will determine whether the acts serve to improve the journey in the direction you are headed.

If you are a recovering addict yet still find yourself surrounded by practicing addicts, it is like being that person at the pool party that's not trying to get wet. Your addict friends will show their love with gifts of drugs and/or alcohol. For any gift giver, to relinquish something that they cherish and gift it to another can be one of the highest forms of altruism. Knowing that it is impolite to reject someone's gift, you may find yourself positioned for a possible relapse into bad behavior. I have found myself several of times eating food that I did not like, indulging in conversations that I was not particularly interested in, and neglecting responsibilities, all in the name of politeness. You should never be selfless at the expense of yourself. Such relationships that call for that are good candidates for review. Typically, healthy relationships are mutually beneficial, and sacrifices made by the individual only adds to the cohesion of the whole.

Take a look at how you are spending "quality time" with the people in your life. The saying goes that "time stands still for no one". In today's society, it is as if time is on fast forward, and if you blink twice, you might miss something. We are bombarded with distractions from every angle, from the streets and prison alike. Activities such as watching TV, playing video games, drugging, and eating, should be scrutinized when opting to spend quality time with one another. One would argue that these activities are harmless and are actually bringing joy to their life. And that, I will not dispute at all. But what is the quality of these activities and are they worth the time spent doing them is the question I would pose. We all must set aside time to relax and interact with others because it is in our nature as human beings.

Absence of social interactions have been found to negatively affect the human psyche. This has been an established observance made in the study of maximum-security prisoners who have spent extended periods in isolation. Therefore, you should evaluate how the quality time you spend, adds to your quality of life. Why not instead of eating out with your friend every weekend, you switch it up? Go for a walk. Instead of playing basketball on the video game, go outside and pick up a real ball. Building or reconstructing your relationships quality time around physical activity is one of many ways of cultivating a healthy lifestyle. Getting up and moving around will be something that you look forward to because you will be doing it with the people that you care about. Today's society is designed to accommodate the sedentary lifestyle. All of our needs are being met with little to no effort required. Social media, and video calls, however convenient, have deluded us into believing that this human to human disconnect is normal. They say, "It takes a village to raise a child." I would add that same village is needed to sustain an adult. It is nearly impossible to recognize an individual apart from the group that they belong. The adages abound on this subject, "Birds of a feather flock together," "Two cannot move unless both agree," and "You are the company you keep", just to name a few. Many like myself have found themselves in prison because of a poor choice of company. The people we choose to spend that "quality time" with will inevitably contribute to the quality of our lives.

Those who we are opting to surround ourselves with are our advisers. We confide in them, seeking advice because their opinions are the most valuable to us, believing that they have our best interest at heart. In determining who we elect to advise us, we must first put their lives under the microscope. It's not wise to get your tax advice from the tax evader, nor is it wise to attend yoga classes at the sumo house. Are your advisers happy, healthy, and honorable? We need people around us who approach life with enthusiasm and optimism, not trepidation and pessimism. Those who become excited by your success are paramount in motivating you to take chances and keep up the good work. Multiple advisers will assist you in multiple areas according to their strengths. The Pope may not be able to help you get that beach body is all I'm saying. The quality of their character is of the utmost importance as well. Honesty is a necessity. Self-destructive people surround themselves with sycophants, and yes men in efforts to avoid a difficult confrontation with the truth. These ill advisers will buy you that drink knowing you have already had one too many, talk you into rather than out of a bad decision, tell you look good in that dress, and support anything else you do, right or wrong. The sage adviser is not afraid to hurt your feelings if it boils down to your feelings or the truth. They are not enablers, and don't help to reinforce destructive behaviors.

5

When we analyze the actions apart from the people doing them, it becomes easy to label someone as good or bad as if the subject is Black or white with no gray area in between. That gray area is exactly where some of our most cherished people reside. A lot of misguidance is given to use mistakenly packaged as love, coupled with ignorance. Is an attentive parent or spouse skilled enough to ignore the pleas of their loved one when they bawl out in anguish over the pangs of withdrawal? It would be unfair to expect them to comport themselves with the same composure as a seasoned drug counselor. Nevertheless, what is fair or unfair, just, or unjust is of little consequence in reference to the quality of someone's life. The only decision we are left with is to properly choose our team, not basing our decisions on familiarities or antiquated history. But rather the sheer will to optimize the quality of your life.

Places/Spaces

One might ask me; how could you possibly change your places in prison? Supermax was distinctly designed for prisoners to have no control over their movements. Many cannot stay out of trouble even if trouble was hiding from them, and for them, prison has become somewhat of a refuge. Preventing violence by way of isolation among other restrictions. Yet even under these conditions, trouble is always made available to the persistent. Therefore, we must conclude that if it is possible to continually find trouble under the strictest conditions, then we may need to approach changing our places in an entirely new way. I cannot over emphasize the fact that regardless of being a prisoner or civilian, people make bad decisions which put us in worse places. There may be a large gap between sitting in the getaway car at a bank robbery and sitting in on a gossip fest about Tom, Dick, and/or Harry. Yet the one thing they have in common is faulty thinking. Just because one act is more extreme than the other does not mean that similarities, cannot be drawn. When it comes to the places and spaces that we find ourselves in, you would be surprised by how different a place can be made to look, solely by changing your thinking. People seldom realize that they occupy different places at the same time. How is that possible you ask. Well permit me to explain. At any given moment we find ourselves situated in a particular location. Whether it be in the store shopping, outside jogging, or in the cell reading this book. There you exist in all your physicality, taking up your specific amount of space. But – what's all that activity in your head? Our minds bounce around from place to place, unrestricted to visit the past, present, or future. Simultaneously, we function in the physical world and the world as we perceive it. Few people have mastered the ability to be fully present in the moment and receive the world as it is. Many including myself, process the world through our individual filters. By the time the world reaches us, it is significantly distorted often by trauma, fear, insecurities, and the like. When these distortions are allowed to run rampant, going unchecked, they often lead us to undesirable places. First our mental spaces must be improved upon before we can see some tangible results. But as with everything, there is a positive side to our filters unless we have desires to become some levitating monk in the mountains somewhere, untethered by the woes of daily life. It is more realistic to work towards viewing the world through a positive filter.

Let's imagine that you are a first-grade schoolteacher. You are surrounded by twenty plus animated, energetic, seemingly unruly six-year-olds. Unless you have plans to retire soon, this will be your life for a while. Unable to change your location, how do you keep from pulling your hair out and going insane? The only thing you can control in these moments is your thinking. You have the option to look around and see a pack of hellions running amuck, or you can choose to see the uncultivated potential of a future generation. The latter perspective sounds like a no brainer on paper but is by no means an easy mental shift to make in the moment. As with every skill that is acquired, thinking positively requires continuous effort and repetition until it becomes second nature. Plenty of brothers that I have spoken with while in prison have commented that they "want to go to another prison" or "when they go home, they are leaving Baltimore." In assessing the statements, I always try to discover the intent behind the relocation. Regarding the transfer to another prison, you typically will hear that their motivation is gaining more accessibility to the things that will extend their stay. Then there is leaving Baltimore, as if they are in the passenger seat of their lives and Baltimore is the driving force of their demise. Do you know the common denominator in anyone's relocation? Themselves! You can go anywhere you want in the world, but you have to take you with you. Until the overhaul is done on your mind, you will arrive at every destination with the same faulty thinking. The more you change your thought patterns the more you may come to realize that it could be less about you changing your places, and more about changing your mind set in those places. Don't get me wrong, there are definitely "no fly zone" places that you simply should not venture into. But the wonderful thing is that once you adjust your thinking, these dangerous areas become more perceptible, thus avoidable. You will be able to determine (not in hindsight but in real-time) whether a conversation, a destination, or even a thought is conducive to the direction you want your life to be headed. Constant vigilance of the places that we, along with our mind occupy is an essential step in improving the quality of your life.

THINGS

The things that we associate with naturally coincide with the people and places in our lives. Things can be objects or ideas. They are inanimate and have no tangible power on their own. Take gold, or oil as an example. For thousands of years, mankind has waged war over the control of natural resources. Lives have been lost and societies destroyed in the name of things. Things, that although many have tried, cannot be taken with them after death. So, what is this apparent obsession with things that have led to the destruction of so many? For most people, it is as if "things" take on a life of their own. They become endowed with such sentimental value, that it renders the possessor incapable of imagining life without it. This obsessive attachment to things, we have labeled as an addiction. There is a litany of things that people have managed to become addicted to. The most popular addictions we see in the 21st century is to drugs, alcohol, and food. Although the list may be long with others, these three receive extra attention because of their proven connection to poor health and death. Addicts show up in the world in many different ways. Addiction is broadly defined as persistent compulsive use of a substance known by the user to be harmful. Some addicts' addictions take on either a biological or psychological dependency, but often times, it's a combination of both. Abusers of alcohol and opioids like heroin have a far more complicated journey to recovery than most. Simply because the body develops a dependency all the way down to a molecular level and to quit (cold turkey) without the assistance of a licensed professional can be potentially life threatening. Aside from that, here we can start to unpack some of the psychological factors that lead to our attachment and addiction to harmful things. In my adolescence, I was like many of my peers, a champion for marijuana. You would find yourself ensnared in a heated debate if you tried to convince one that marijuana was a gateway drug. Now, reflecting back on those times, I would say that these arguments were only made to justify my poor lifestyle choices. Upon entering high school at the age of fourteen, the first thing I ever smoked was marijuana. Naturally followed cigarettes, alcohol, and ecstasy. All within a month. Of course, you will have those that will argue that they smoke or have smoked marijuana and it never led to the abuse of anything else. I applaud those who are able to profess that, because in my experience, they are unicorns. Those rare exceptions are always used as the poster children of marijuana advocacy. The plant itself, I agree can be beneficial because of its medicinal properties, but the majority of its use is for recreational purposes. As I said before, we empower "things." Thus, in the case of marijuana, this herb has long standing ties to the substance abuse community. What makes marijuana a gateway drug in my opinion, is the associated behavior that must be adopted once use begins. For me, it introduced me to a lot of people who I would have otherwise had no reason to talk to. I began to adopt a deceptive mindset, in order to hide my use from my parents. I skipped school, neglected my responsibilities, and lost genuine friends, all for the love of marijuana. This new lifestyle that many are lured into by seemingly harmless marijuana, is "what makes marijuana a gateway drug. We mustn't be deceived by the burgeoning acceptance, and legalization. A great example of a legal gateway drugs is what has now been termed as the Opioid Epidemic. America's minority communities have wrestled with addiction to heroin for over half a century, which is closely associated with opioids. Yet it wasn't until opioid and heroin use invaded the middle and upper-class households, that they became considered an epidemic worthy of observation. This gateway the people are lead through from legal opioid medications to heroin is even more ominous than marijuana. A person may suffer an injury to their back for example. They are subsequently prescribed pain medications. Effective as they may be at alleviating the pain, the euphoria felt can become highly addictive after extended use of these medications. This level of addiction as I mentioned before is beyond a psychological addiction and the individual has now become physically dependent on the medication as well. The extent of that dependency is easily overlooked as long as the doctor is continually writing those prescriptions and the pharmacist is filling them. But what do you think happens when their prescription can no longer be filled. You might have a few that will throw their hands up and say "Hey" I had a nice run, but it's all over now." But for many, it becomes time to plot, plan, and strategize how they will get their fix. Now they have crossed through the gateway and are in the express lane to destruction. They may begin their journey by illegally purchasing pills wherever they can find them, but many soon discover that the pills are just a little too expensive as well as difficult to acquire. It should be stated that "All opioid roads lead to heroin." To an addict, it makes absolute sense to make the transition from prescription pills to heroin. Heroin is cheaper, you get higher, and it is more accessible. So, the question is not if, but when the transition will be made.

Alcohol is yet another legal substance that often progresses to the point of abuse. Drinking is promoted as a social act, in which many television commercials depict young and old

Ryan M. McLean

people alike having a good time with their drinks in hand. I guess a commercial depicting a homeless person living in squalor because of their alcoholism would not be a good marketing ploy. But it would be honest. The things that lead to our destruction could never be marketed objectively. When you see the latest drug commercial, I guarantee you that you will be able to walk away knowing exactly how it can benefit you. A lot of money goes into making sure you fully comprehend the product in the little bit of time it airs. But little time and effort are put into explaining the seemingly endless list of side effects. I must emphasize how important it is to come to know exactly what effects the things we ingest have on our body, especially when it comes to food. The foods we choose to eat as well as the foods that we lack; all contribute to our overall health. People like me were never properly taught in our adolescence about the relationship that food has with the body. The quality of our lives is directly impacted according to what we are consuming. In more recent years, access to nutritional information is at our fingertips. With a Google search you can find an abundance of recipes, diets, and magic weight loss programs. So, why with all of this information available are we seeing increases in obesity, and other food related health issues? This is because, in most developed countries, accompanied with that development is abundance. Abundance of all thing's food related. Speaking from my experience as a first generation Jamaican American, I can tell you that my relatives from Jamaica and Jamaicans in general do not have the same abusive relationship with food that we have here in the States. My Father often tells stories of his upbringing in Jamaica and his eating patterns in those times. He says that he used to believe that he was malnourished because he never had the opportunity to eat steak and other types of red meat like in the States. He grew up in a place

12

where he ate more fruits and vegetable then he did meat. All of which was locally grown. The processed foods were simply not as prevalent in Jamaica as is America. In his time spent in Jamaica, he was in the best shape of his life. After he immigrated to America, you could see the decline in his health. A Jamaican will tell you that you are doing good if you're fat. Attributing your weight gain to your new-found prosperity. So, in Jamaican terms, my dad was "doing good", but the doctor didn't agree with that sentiment. He found himself overweight and taking diabetes and high blood pressure medications for ailments that he acquired since he started "doing good." Many will attribute weight gain, and the decline of their health as just another part of the aging process. It is true that with age, cells begin deteriorating. This deterioration is the cause of the wrinkles we begin to form as we age, the graying and loss of hair, as well as loss of muscle mass. All good things must come to a end one day, yet we accelerate the process with our poor eating habits. A lot of foods and beverages that we consume shave years off our lives while simultaneously reducing the quality of the time that we have left. Changing the way that we think about food, coupled with the quality and quantity that we consume is essential to leading an overall healthy lifestyle.

Considering people, places, and things in light of all that we have discussed. This should assist you in identifying the messy areas of your life that could use some improvement. Always bear in mind that we live in extraordinary times. A time where chaos is promoted as normal, and structure and discipline viewed as an infringement on one's freedom. To fail to make that observation is to improperly prepare for the journey ahead. A lifelong journey of vigilance and good decision making are our only defenses when trying to live a healthy lifestyle.

Chapter 2

Routines and Habits

Many see the word habit and automatically approach it defensively. When the word bad is mentioned, habit often follows closely behind. A habit is defined as a behavior pattern acquired by frequent repetition or physiologic exposure that shows itself in regularity or increased facility of performance. Simply put, habits are not innately "bad." I believe the reason why habits are so closely associate with negativity is because there is a lot of negativities in the world. There also is a lot of good, but the good seldom makes the headlines. At the end of an hour-long news program, they reserve five minutes to tell you about the good being done in the world. So, if habits are being acquired by repetition, it should be no wonder that we acquire bad habits the same way from the repeated exposure to negativity and misbehavior and we become desensitized to the trauma being done to us. Our routines are reflective of our habits. Typically, our routines are the foundation of our daily life. Routine has been defined as a habitual or mechanical performance of an established procedure. Day after day we partake in activities that are described as entertainment. But what does that entertainment look like and what effect does it have on your life? For me growing up, music was a big contributor to some of my bad habits. Music being one of the most frequently consumed products in the world, one can see how it must have an impact on one's life. The utterances of ideas accompanied by melodic rhymes, repeatedly drilled into one's head can almost be trance inducing. These ideas and ideals become our own. I can only speak for myself and for those whom I relate, but I do find it hard to believe that someone can listen to music without being influenced in some type of way. The songs people listen to can give you an idea of what's on their mind. As for myself, it was a lot of street music that always reinforced the habits of the streets. Hanging out with friends, chasing money and women, while indulging in drugs and alcohol was part of the routine. I would say that those aspects of my life were a lot more consistent than others. I had no consistent routine when it came to school, work, money, eating, or exercise. I had managed to properly organize my destructive behavioral patterns while neglecting the things that should have been of importance.

We have a way of prioritizing fun, as to assure that we are having it all the time and put little effort into adding structure in those still untamed areas of our lives. A well-constructed routine is essential to the goal oriented individual. When you have an understanding of who you are, who you want to be, and where you want to be in your life, it is easier to put the things in place to get you there. Once you have decided on a destination, you must avoid all behavior that is moving contrary to where you are headed. All journeys to adopt healthy habits and routines are typically long and arduous. We are often so deeply invested in our bad behavior that it takes an equal amount of time to completely form your ideal habits. Don't think it strange that you still crave that beer after a long day of work, even though it's been a year since you've had one. Your mind is screaming to you that something is wrong and out of place. The mind craves consistency and uniformity because it alleviates the pressure of micromanaging every little detail of your daily life. With a good routine, the mind can operate on auto pilot, and give more energy to the most important affairs. Organizing every area of your life will continually have that calming effect. When things are disorganized, you naturally will have to dedicate more time and brain power to figuring out what to do at a moment's notice.

Therefore, you must create routines from the largest, all the way down to the smallest areas of your life, and from the moment you wake up to the time you go to sleep. Also, prepare for the sudden change of plans that will potentially disrupt your routine. Beware of an over structured life that has little flexibility. That would be shifting from one extreme to another. Without balance, things boarder on control issues. Prison has a way of bringing that extreme out of people. It is typically most noticeable within the cell, where people can exercise the most influence on their environment. Behaviors ranging from excessive cleanliness to excessive organization within such a small, shared space between two people can be a recipe for disaster. It is a must that people occupying the same space are willing to compromise. Although prison is an extreme and unnatural environment, the same rules apply for people in society as well. We see deadly disputes over parking spaces, property, and possessions every day. This is why, when creating routines and developing habits, it is important that we recognize that the only thing we can control is ourselves. How are we showing up in the world, and what impact are our habits having on the quality of our life? On my journey of self-improvement, a few things come to mind, that I indulged in which went contrary to my desired destination. My drinking was one. Although I drank not nearly as frequently as I once did on the streets, it hadn't yet come to a complete halt. I find a lot of truth in the saying that "Old habits die hard." It's difficult to change a habit if you don't first address the purpose for its development. For some, the reasons may be obvious and for others like myself, you must do some soul searching. In my search, I realized that my drinking along with many of my other bad habits were connected to my desire to fit in and feel accepted. I don't care how much your parents love on you and are present, that desire for your peers' acceptance will always remain. The rejection I felt started at an early age, probably before I could walk and talk. My beloved big brother Ruben seemed to have hated my guts. He and I have explored this topic extensively and I now know that the way he treated me was less about me and more about the personal things he was dealing with. All of that is nice to know in hindsight, but at the time my feelings were my feelings. The closest person to me, only separated by two and a half years, had wanted nothing to do with me. I used to beg him to let me play video games with him and my pleas would be answered with shouts to "Get out his room!" Sometimes my persistence prevailed, and he said I could watch him play as long as I would shut up and not say anything. As sad as it sounds, the time spent watching him play the game are some of my fondest memories of us. With age, my world expanded and my peer group along with it. Like a lot of kids, you meet people and friendships are formed. The same was true for me, but that sense of inadequacy remained. My early experiences with my brother taught me that sometimes you have to be someone other than yourself for others to accept you. That understanding led to skipping school, fighting, drug abuse, and gang affiliation. The habits I adopted, afforded and maintained a particular type of lifestyle. Albeit misguided and destructive, it temporarily alleviated my loneliness.

The thing is, when we sacrifice one part of ourselves to improve the quality of another, it still leaves us fractured, just in a different area. Let's look at prescription medication once again for an example. It is seldom you will find a medication that doesn't have any side effects. The medication will purport to be able to fix one problem while potentially causing a litany of others. Developing habits and creating routines can function in the same way. We see a lot of eating disorders developing out of these attempts to address trauma by the micromanagement of food. On one end of an extreme you will find anorexia nervosa which is defined as a serious disorder in eating behavior primarily of young women in their teens and early twenties that is characterized especially by a pathological fear of weight gain leading to faulty eating patterns, malnutrition,[1] and unusually excessive weight loss. On the other, there is bulimia and overeating. Usually followed by self-induced vomiting or laxative or diuretic abuse and is often accompanied by guilt and depression. Then you have overeating, which is the act of eating to excess, a behavioral pattern that often leads to excessive weight gain and other underlying health issues. These eating disorders are often the physical manifestation of deeper emotional issues.

Naturally then, we have "unfinished business" and we tend to find ways of avoiding the issues in the belief that they will go away. But the issues never go away until you decide to address them. The person who knows what signs to look for when detecting trauma, will view anger, depression, drug abuse, eating disorders and the like as secondary behavioral patterns that stem from deeper rooted issues.

In prison one is presented a unique opportunity to study a plethora of personalities. The most important factor is that the prisoner is not just a mere observer of human behavior. It is an interpersonal experience. I have had to learn how to navigate the many personalities around me, in order to make any progress through the system. What I have learned throughout my incarceration is that during my observation of the behavior of others, it turns out that no one else's behavior, and personality should undergo more scrutiny than my own. Proper navigation does not solely require that you observe the shifting tides of the ocean. You must also make sure that your ship is well equipped to confront the turbulence that the ocean brings. The two physical altercations I engaged in, in the early years of my incarceration, stemmed from me trying to avoid confrontation rather than learning how to appropriately address a situation. On the streets, avoidance is perfectly practical because it is easier to put distance between yourself and the people you don't get along with. Thus, never being forced to confront the issue directly. Now prison on the other hand can be a bit tricky. Avoidance in this environment can cause turmoil that disrupts your entire routine. The issues you have with another may deter you from entering areas of exercise and entertainment, ultimately making your life so miserable that a confrontation is seemingly inevitable. Of course, addressing an issue once you have reached this point will not turn out well for anyone. It is important to honor your emotions by acknowledging their existence and finding the vocabulary that will allow you to give voice to them. Both of my incidents had miscommunication at its root. Making a habit of expressing how you feel, who you are, and what you will and will not accept will assist you in properly addressing situations, rather than letting them build up.

It doesn't take much to create the routines that will improve the quality of your life. Yet it appears that people have the most difficulty with creating routines that will develop good fitness and nutrition habits. Some of the biggest mistakes that I see people make are firstly, having expectations. It is natural to have expectations when you start your fitness journey, but my advice is to get rid of all preconceived notions of what your journey should look like and how long it should take. Fitness and nutrition is a lifelong marathon and assigning time lines and weight loss goals are fast ways to become discouraged. What I am saying goes contrary to popular belief. Weight loss programs are designed around the scale. They promise a certain amount of weight loss in a certain amount of time. Most people have that magic number that they have concocted in their head, and that if they could just reach it everything would be perfect. Let me tell you the problem about this way of thinking. Whenever someone refers to health, they speak in terms of "Being." "Being" healthy or "Being" unhealthy. This "Being" the case, why do we try to "DO" healthy? "Being" speaks to one's existence and gives me the impression that it is less about what goal you reach or how much muscle you build and more about your commitment to continually do what it takes to be healthy, with no finish line in sight. By adopting this perspective of what health looks like, it takes some of the pressure off and allows you to just "be". You will be taken by surprise by the results that you achieve without investing the conscious effort you thought it took. Next, I would caution against beginning your journey with a partner. Although they say "Teamwork makes the dream work" and all that good stuff, partners can become a big obstacle for the undisciplined. When the partnership is functioning like a well-oiled machine, it makes it easy to stay focused and make progress. But, when one partner breaks the routine for whatever reason, it can be disastrous for both individuals. This is your life you are dealing with, and you have to be able to hold yourself accountable. In prison, it is easy to fall into the habit of relying on workout partners to get in shape. The abundance of free time also makes it easier to maintain a workout partnership. Yet, as I have said before, people are people regardless of where you go. Whether prison or the streets, people have things to do and their own priorities that may not align with those of another. Now you find a situation where because one partner is not available to workout, the other makes that an excuse for them not to do anything. It will continually be restated throughout this book that the only thing we can control is ourselves. Flexibility must be the foundation of your routine, where regardless of what you had planned and who you planned it with, you will not be rendered useless and still muster the ability to move forward with doing the things necessary to improve your life. Most importantly, if you plan on getting healthy and staying healthy, you have to make sure that your motivations are sustainable. Everything we do serves a purpose and some of those purposes have a longer shelf life than others. Athletes are the best example of how someone can be motivated to stay in shape because their health and fitness is a requirement for them to be able to perform to the best of their ability. After their retirement, we often see a drastic change in their lifestyle. Being at peak performance is no longer essential and now they feel as though they can relax. That relaxation is actually a person deciding to relax on their discipline and foregoing healthy behavioral patterns in exchange for chaotic and unhealthy ones. Typically leading to weight gain and an accelerated decline in health. Therefore, when one's occupation does not require athleticism, we are called to become more creative to our fitness and nutrition approach. This will involve spending more time getting to know yourself and how your body works. You will learn how to develop habits and create routines that will be sustainable and propel you further on your lifelong journey.

Chapter 3

Purpose

I think purpose is an important attribute to have in one's life, so much so that I felt it necessary to write a chapter on the subject.

Purpose is an essential aspect of everything we do, whether we realize it or not. The French have so eloquently termed it "le raison d'etre" literally meaning the reason for being. Purpose can also be synonymous with intention. Purpose is your motivation, goal, aim, desire, your reason for going to bed, and waking up. As the French said, your reason for being. Many faiths believe human beings were created by God to serve a purpose. Regardless of what you believe in, this fact alone shows that the idea of purpose has been around for thousands of years.

We make it difficult on ourselves when we don't recognize the power of purpose in our lives. Failing to identify purpose leaves you in a state of simply existing. Arbitrarily moving through life being guided by a whim, like rolling the dice and leaving our lives up to chance. Interestingly enough, there are more people than not who live their lives this way. So, you can imagine how the circumstances a person is born into could direct their life if they do not possess the awareness of purposes' power. A lot of times we allow the outside influences to inspire or dissuade us from doing the things that interest us. The goal in life should not be solely to be able to unrestrictedly follow our interests. For our interests are often momentary and constantly changing. The goal should be to create a quality, and productive life that is assisted by the things that interest us. Productivity and success should go hand in hand with our interests. Without the two in mind, we open the door to allowing ourselves to be interested in destructive activities that end up taking from us more than they give. The number one thing to consider is the time we invest in the things we do. There is no slowing down or rewinding the clock. Spending hours, days, weeks, months, and years on things that are not adding to the quality of your life is one way we live purposelessly. How often do we spend time considering the future? This day and age promotes living for today and not worrying about tomorrow, hence the acronym "Yolo (you only live once)". When you approach life in this manner, you may not be prepared for the curve balls that life will throw you.

Coming up as a child, I used to ask a million questions, and frankly still do. Some people use to discourage me from asking questions so, one day I went to my father exclaiming that "people say I ask too many dumb questions". He told me "There's no such thing as a dumb question, only a dumb answer". Still to this day, he encourages me to question everything done, or said, as well as why things exist or why something doesn't exist. This inquisitive nature was eventually directed upon me. It took me coming to prison to decide to ask myself some serious questions. Who am I? Is this question simmering under the surface, waiting to be answered by us all.

Interestingly enough, I am the only one to have ever posed the question to myself. The question emerged after listening to several people in court, whom I had never met, explain who

I am and what I was about to a jury. Was I that guy that they were describing? No! Then what am I doing here and what have I been doing for them to even think of me in this light? I had to put my life under the same scrutiny that the State of Maryland was putting me under. They do not know me, but do I know me? It is amazing how posing the right questions to yourself can send you on a journey that you never come back from. The questions do not come all at once or in any particular order, they arise as you travel, forcing you to assign purpose and meaning to the routes you are on.

Life is not linear by any stretch of the imagination, and throughout it, we wear many different hats. Simply put, we find ourselves headed in many different directions, directed by different interests and events. If you are anything like me, the constant change in direction can be a bit disorienting. You find yourself doing this, that, and the other, and ultimately not completing anything. I have been advised to slow down and focus on one or two things. My mentor reminded me of the saying that goes "A Jack of all trades and a master of none." The advice of our most trusted advisers should not be overlooked" but you also must be the architect of your own life.

Maximizing your productivity, should not be the same as stifling your growth. Opportunities to expand your knowledge or grow in a particular area may present themselves at inopportune times. So, do you forgo an opportunity because you are devoting your time to something else? I believe in taking advantage of your advantages. This is where prioritization comes into play. Now you have an opportunity to test out your organizational skills. Make a list, ordering it by importance. The most important being number one and the least coming last. Certain activities must be done at a certain time. The time with the duration of the activity should be added to the list.

Absent of putting some serious thought into prioritizing our lives will leave us feeling overwhelmed. The most common complaint is that there are just not enough hours in a day to get everything done. Here in prison, there has been several times where I have asked brothers, why they weren't tackling a project that they previously had mentioned they wanted to complete. The go to excuse is that they are too busy working on their case. It sounds good and it is a quick way to silence your inquirer when he is attempting to hold you accountable. Yet the fact of the matter is that no one is going to be incessantly doing the same thing, hour after hour, day after day. Yea, what you are doing may be important, but everything has a time frame. Sometimes we must take a step back from the task at hand in order to more effectively resume our work at a later date. This does not mean ceasing all activity but rather investing your time and energy in another area on your list. Fill those spaces of idle time with activities that could be accomplished in the same amount of time. You would be surprised to see how much time is actually spent doing nothing. Isn't it amazing how the busiest amongst us always manage to carve out some time to watch TV. Time spent watching TV does not have to be a complete waste of time. Unless you are a celebrity movie critic or watching something educational that demands a hundred percent of your attention, there are things you can do while watching your programs. In an supermax security prison, the majority of our time is spent in front of the television. It is hard to escape the distraction that TV brings. I know some very disciplined Muslim brothers who have opted to get rid of their televisions in order to be more focused. For most, that is too extreme and impractical. Instead of depriving yourself completely of something you enjoy, locate those activities that can be done in tandem with your screen time. Over the years I have found that both exercise and study can take place while you enjoy the idiot box. Exercises like squats, step ups, weightlifting, treadmill, and stationary bike can all be done without turning your head from the screen. The television becomes a welcome distraction when performing these activities because it enables you to worry less about the task at hand and lends more of your attention, to the program. I caution against performing any activity that requires 100 percent of your attention, you may increase your potential for injury. When selecting things to study during these times, you should choose materials that are easily comprehensible. Something that does not require much more than a glance at a time will give you the optimal experience of both activities. As for myself, a passion and hobby of mine is learning languages. What the study of languages has taught me is that your undivided attention should be given to learning the grammatical rules to a given language. After that comes the long but easy part of language learning. At this point, with word order understood, all you have to do is memorize words and build up your vocabulary. New words can be learned with a glance and your TV show goes uninterrupted. I believe by finding more productive activities to do while watching TV will allow you to better utilize your time and ultimately improve your quality of life. Purpose must be considered beyond merely what we do. How much time do you devote to just "being."

Who we are is essential to directing our intentions. Our desires, motivations, and passions are all reflective of our character. How much time is spent contemplating your values? They exist for everyone and are often a product of our upbringing. Once established in those times, we seldom do the work of evaluating them and possibly changing them. To challenge one's values is almost like challenging everything they know to be true. This is especially difficult when the particular value was acquired from and modeled after a loved one. I was fortunate to have two amazing parents, who always functioned as an efficient team. The only area that I can critique is the value that was placed upon food, as well as the amount of trust that was afforded my brother and me. My parents are the most trustworthy people I know and that is part of the foundation that they built their relationship on. I am an extension of them, and I am expected to move as such. When I would find myself in trouble at school, I never quite understood what my farther meant when he said that I was a representation of them. You will undoubtedly develop some shared values with people closest to you. My parent's confidence in me enabled me to at times be deceptive and associate with questionable characters. Naturally, I started to become not only a representation of my parents but also my peers. After my incarceration, all of the friends from whom I developed my destructive values, had turned their backs on me. The abandonment was upsetting at first, but then I soon realized that I was presented an opportunity to disassociate with the values that I had previously acquired. Whenever you are operating with a faulty value system, life will reveal it to you. It is just up to you to listen. The advantage that my parents gave me cannot be understated. It is harder to do better if you don't know better. The one thing we are all adept at doing is spotting success. Of course, success is in the eye of the beholder, where each individual will see it exemplified differently. Without good judgment and foresight, it is easy to become attracted to the instant gratification that criminality brings. Overnight success has always been a topic of much discussion, no matter how shady it may be. Documentary after documentary, we learn about the rise and fall of some criminal enterprise. It is always the fall that is least emphasized. All the ignorant take away is what to do to not get caught. True success is sustainable. Most of the time it is not achieved overnight and is a long and arduous process. This is why key morals and principles must be developed in order to be able to enjoy real success. If we do not equip ourselves with the proper temperament required to choose virtue over vice, how can we expect to experience the things we say we want in life? I have yet to come across someone who says it was their intention to come to prison. You have some crazy and wicked people out there, but everyone I have ever had deep conversations with, had some type of ambition. No matter how distorted their perception, they always believed that their actions would somehow improve the quality of their life.

It is possible to build a house without a foundation. Just prepare for the walls to collapse on you. But a house built on a solid foundation will provide you with the resources necessary for true purpose to emerge.

Chapter 4

Treat Yourself Don't Cheat Yourself

We view taking care of ourselves as one of the worst punishments one could inflict on themselves. The word diet in and of itself appears to have a negative connotation to it. Far too often it turns out that our health is simply not a good enough reason to stop eating and doing the things we love. This is the reason we see people with lung cancer still smoking and obese people still overeating. It is easy to look on the surface of one's life and observe the problems that need fixing, but much more effort is required to get to the root cause of destructive behavior. As we have previously discussed, there are a litany of factors that attribute to one's health. In this section I will be mainly discussing our eating habits. The reason for this is because the relationship we have with food, is and always will be the longest lasting relationship we will ever have. The relationships we have with drugs and alcohol, or friends and family can come and go, but good old nourishment will be your companion from the beginning to the end. Just like any relationship, your relationship with food can be nurturing and invigorating or toxic and antagonistic. If you think I'm joking, just look at some of the ways we describe food. We all have used the expression that some type of food is "calling us." I don't know how it always manages to get our number. Or what about when "something has your name on it" and I'm not talking about a birthday cake. We take possession of the food even before it is prepared. Many interpret love or hospitality according to how they share their food. Every culture has different rules and customs when it comes to consumption of food. I believe our ancestors had very good understanding of the importance of a healthy relationship with food. Just like with anything, if there are no rules and regulations that govern one's conduct, things typically spiral towards abuse. America as well as other developed Nations has become something like the Wild West when it comes to food. Becoming frontiers of unrestricted exploit and abuse of food. My cellmate and I were watching BET one day and began to become frustrated about the length and frequency at which the commercials were displayed. We timed them and for every six minutes of regular programming came six minutes of commercials. A majority of which were food commercials. Unknowingly, we are lulled into a trance in which we meditate, and concentrate on food, night and day. Anything given too much attention can become an obsession, and it is as if we are willingly obsessing over food. As I have mentioned before, this obsession can lead to anxiety, and eating disorders. It has been said that once an addict always an addict, regardless of the length of time since you last used. Although I indulged in drugs and alcohol for a small portion of my life, it was surprisingly easy to quit. Once I decided that my life would benefit greatly from the absence of those dependencies, the good times promised by my drugs of choice had lost their appeal. I wish the same could be said about food. The saying goes that "We should eat to live and not live to eat." If that could be put into practice, we would find the solution to many of our problems. As I have mentioned plenty of times already, food is one of those inescapable necessities and because of this need for nourishment, it is an area easy to exploit. One cannot wake up one day and say you know what, "I'm quitting food". You might even sincerely feel that way in the moment you say it (probably because you are over-stuffed from the night before), but the moment you use the bathroom and clear up some space, you quickly forget about your former sentiment. Then with the aid of good old advertisement, you are directed to your nearest fast-food restaurant to take advantage of their new special. I would say that one blessing that has come out of my incarceration is my inaccessibility to fast food. Fast food took up a huge portion of my life up until the day I got lock up. Aside from eating it since I grew teeth in my mouth, I also had the opportunity to work in three different restaurants from the age of fourteen to just barely eighteen. Wendy's, McDonalds, and Burger King gave me the opportunity to improve my relationship with fast food. If not for the simultaneous drug use during that time, I probably would have gained a substantial amount of weight, but often times I didn't have an appetite. But when I did! I was like a tornado in there. I had access to everything and rarely had to spend a dime. So, had I not gotten incarcerated, I possibly would have worked my way into owning my own franchise and ate my way into some serious health problems by now. This prison experience has really illuminated my understanding of fast foods effects on the body. Absent of it, one immediately sees improvements in their skin, weight, digestive system, and many other aspects of your overall health. But for many in prison, this absence is just another punishment, and they dream of the day they can get out and frequent their favorite fast-food joint. I have yet to have the pleasure of getting released from prison, for this is my first incarceration, but I have been told several stories about other brothers released from a former incarceration. You wouldn't believe how for many of them, the first thing they did upon their release was stopping at a fast-food spot. Now this is a teachable moment for those who don't know. After going for an extended period without fast food, your body had begun healing itself. Finally, being able to find respite from the constant bombardment of junk food, the body wakes up from its toxic food induced stupor and begins to get its affairs in order. Then you decide to flood it, once again with all that poison it just got finished healing from. The body will put up a fight initially, causing you to have some serious bouts of diarrhea. This is the body's way of telling you that something is wrong and attempting to expel its content as quickly as possible. But of course, we ignore our body's pleas to stop what we are doing. In our mind, the body just needs some time to get back to normal. Eventually, the body realizes that this is the best it's going to get and learns to survive in a toxic environment: Unhappy as it may be, what other choice does it have?

If we look at our body as an entity separate from ourselves or rather a friend or significant other, it will give us a better idea of how we are treating it. When we don't take care of our bodies, they don't take care of us. Listening, nurturing, being considerate, protecting, and countless other qualities that you would apply to a relationship must be applied to yourself. When your body is not cooperating with you, that is a good sign that something is off. Sometimes we can be so abusive to our body that our "heart attacks" us. If that's not a toxic relationship, I don't know what is. Yet when the two of you move in harmony, you become one truly efficient team. So, what choices do we have? Many assume that living a healthy lifestyle is not living at all. The belief is that you are "cheating" yourself out of the wonderful experiences in life. If that were actually the case, you would hear no complaints from me, but there is a way we can enjoy the foods we love without compromising our health. Let's begin with a change of perspective. Instead of viewing life from a glass half empty perspective, we must see the glass as half full. So, when it comes to food, you must view the periodic consumption of the foods you love as a treat rather than something you are being deprived of. It would be ideal for the food you love the most to be healthy as well, but this typically is not the case. It is more common for them to be high in sugar, fat, carbs, and overall calories, with little to no nutritional value. These treats are undoubtedly delicious, and it would be ludicrous to expect you to give them up completely. Yet, the mission should be to earn them. I don't care how much you like a thing, too much of it takes away some of the enjoyment. But, when you eat that treat after a long time without it, you enjoy it that much more. Birthday cake is one of my favorite kinds of cake and I don't think I should have to wait for my or someone else's birthday just to have it. But I also have to bear in mind that it's a treat for special occasions. It has been over a decade since I have had birthday cake, but there's a litany of other junk food to take its place. Here in prison, it is easy to adopt poor eating habits. Most of us didn't have good eating habits to begin with, so prison just reinforces these habits. Cakes, cookies, chips, noodles, and a plethora of different meats, all can be purchased from commissary. Like the streets, anything sold that is not outright unhealthy is the most expensive, so you are dissuaded from buying it and opt to buy what is cheaper. This dynamic also re-enforces poor eating coupled with the fact that most are not knowledgeable in reading packaging or simply don't care to. I remember years ago when I was well into my healthy eating journey, I used to eat tuna fish and crackers every night. I thought I was doing pretty good, I looked good, and I felt great. Then one day I got the news that my beloved grandmother had passed away which was a tremendous blow. Coincidently, the next day I had to go see the nurse about my knee. It is routine that whenever you see the nurse, your blood pressure is checked and you are weighed. After taking my blood pressure, the nurse informed me that it was higher than normal. I explained to her that I had been crying the night before and maybe that had something to do with it. She told me that they would be calling me for the next few days to keep an eye on it to see if I needed to be put on medication. That was a completely unexpected turn of events for me. I was twenty-four and in the best shape I had ever been in my life. So how is it that I am now being told that I might need to be medicated? The next day I went, I was told it was still high. I no longer had the crying excuse and now was left perplexed as to why it was so high. I had to do some investigating. I didn't have to look too far because the only thing I ate outside of my three meals a day was tuna fish and crackers. I stopped eating them both and over the next few days of observation, I was told that my pressure had returned to normal and medication would not be necessary. This incident deepened my understanding of nutrition, because for those who have some knowledge of reading packaging, we often only read to see how many calories are in something. It is important to remember that all packaged foods have increased amounts of sodium as opposed to their natural or unpackaged form because the sodium helps to preserve the product. In my case, I was so focused on the fact that the tuna only had 140 calories, 1g of total fat, and 31g of protein that I completely overlooked the fact that it has 480mg of sodium. That paired with crackers that were although also low in calories, had about 150mg of sodium for every 5 crackers. I ate twenty at a time so that put me at 600mg. So, each night I ate 1,080mg worth of sodium in tuna fish and crackers alone, and that is not counting all the other sodium filled foods I ate throughout the day.

2,300 mg is the daily recommended amount of sodium, meaning that I was eating more than half that amount as a snack. For many, especially people of African descent are more susceptible to high blood pressure than others. It also doesn't help that people of African descent make up a large portion of impoverished communities that often rely upon highly processed and preserved foods on a daily basis. These communities are also known as food dessert communities because of their scarcity of affordable, nutritious food. Prison is a de facto impoverished community. The majority of the food we receive comes either from a can or a bag. The fresh fruit and vegetables that we do get are either no longer fresh when they reach us or are so heavily sprayed with pesticides that it makes you hesitant to eat them. Every meal is loaded with cheap white carbs that offer little to no nutritious value. Yet in spite of all these nutritional road 'blocks, it is still possible to lead a healthy lifestyle and enjoy the food you love while doing it. There are small simple alterations you can make to your diet, which I guarantee will cause your body to change immediately. We must first identify the foods we can eat the most frequently. Next, we have to assess what nutritional value these items or meals have. For those who are not adept at reading packaging or do not care to, ·this may present a problem. There are plenty of small items that you would never expect to pack such a powerful punch. For example, I have a small pack of Market Square Bakery Duplex crème cookies in front of me and I can and will undoubtedly eat this whole pack in one sitting. Of course, I'm only speaking for myself but, people don't typically abide by the 5 servings that are indicated in the nutrition facts. It says that there are 140 calories per serving, which is not bad until you realize a serving is only three cookies! Who is going to stop eating after three cookies when the pack has fifteen? So, after we eat all fifteen of the cookies, we then have to multiply that by 140 by 5 because we just ate 5 servings which now is actually 700 calories! I say all that to say, small packages can pack a big punch. I would be surprised if everyone could not point out at least one of these explosive items in their diet. If you are trying to determine everything that is contributing to your unhealthy lifestyle, be sure to take beverages in consideration as well. We Americans consume vast amounts of sugary soft drinks on a daily basis. Sodas are so deeply intertwined with the culture that it has been deemed appropriate to have a soda with every meal and for every occasion. This practice alone can lead to health problems such as diabetes because of the considerable amounts of sugar being consumed on a regular basis. Like I said, sodas are part of the culture. So, I wouldn't ask you to give up something completely that has probably been with you since your childhood, but we can't make this an everyday thing. Therefore, to stave off the misery that will accompany you taking a step back from your lifelong companion, here is my suggestion. Forget about doing the sugar free this and the zero that. Why? Because you are only replacing regular sodas with diet sodas. Number one, nothing replaces the taste of the real thing and second, you are still continuing a bad habit of regular soda consumption. We should place less emphasis on the product and more on our thinking of the product. The problem is not so much that we like sodas. It's the fact that we feel like we have to have one everyday which is the problem. So, the switch from regular to diet does little to break a bad habit. Diet sodas are a slippery slope to the real thing. Imagine you have your daily routine of grabbing that ice-cold diet soda from the vending machine on your lunch break, but today they are all out. What do you do? Drink the ice-cold classic version that is right underneath it? Or do you just walk away empty handed. We are such creatures of habit that I would bet my bottom dollar that you pick the former rather than the latter. The thought process would be, "Well, I've been doing good so far and, one regular soda can't hurt". The thing is, I'm not in disagreeing with that, because to me a soda is a soda regardless as to what you put in it. I am not challenging you to change a product, I am challenging you to change your habits. Treat yourself don't cheat yourself! We are doing ourselves a disservice by two-stepping around the real issue at hand. We cheat ourselves every time we go for the easy fixes, putting band aids on bullet wounds. The most destructive patterns are the hardest to brake. But like I said before, it starts with a change of perspective. I wouldn't stop drinking that classic soda if that was what I truly enjoyed. But that soda is going to have to be like that friend you hang out with on the weekends. You'll have a good time when you come together but you can't make this an everyday thing. This too applies to every other type of junk food. Enjoying the real thing once or twice a week can be more satisfying than having it, or a healthy version of it every day. When you "Treat" yourself this way, you begin to create new habits that will improve your health as well as your enjoyment of your favorite things. I have gained this understanding from dealing with the inconsistencies of prison. In the institution where I am currently housed, we have an opportunity to get commissary once a week. This structure forces you to put a little bit of thought into what you plan to order that will last you until the next week. A lot of people will load up on all the junk foods they like so that they will have access to it whenever they so desire. See, the problem with this is that in your attempt to be properly prepared for the possibility of satisfying a craving that might arise, you wind up snacking all throughout the week because it is readily available. Therefore, I concluded that if I wanted to treat myself in the up-and-coming week, I would select a few items that would not last me longer than a day or two. When they are gone, it's back to business as usual. This restriction on the frequency of which I can order food has permitted me to create a thinking pattern of looking forward to a "treat" once a week. This method can be adopted on the streets. Avoid stocking up your pantry with a bunch of junk food because having that easy access may be a little too enticing. Try making plans for what your treat will be on your "treat day" and get it close to the time you plan to eat it. If you have chosen a particular day to be your "treat day" this will enable you to more easily turn down unhealthy foods during the course of every other day. Remember: This is a lifestyle thing not a diet. Every modification made to our eating habits should be realistic and sustainable. When we take extreme measures (often seeking quick results), we become miserable and disappointed because we are not seeing the immediate results for our big sacrifice, which may convince us to give up all together. Once applying some of these subtle changes in our diets, by removing the unhealthiest items and restricting them to only once or twice a week, we will be on track to leading both a healthy and happy lifestyle.

Chapter 5

The Dreaded Yet Unavoidable

For most people, the common consensus is that they dread the thought of working out. Yes! I said the "thought". It is not so much the act in and of itself that brings about such discomfort, but rather the abundance of discouraging thoughts that accompany it. Let's look at some of the things we think and tell ourselves when entertaining the idea of working out.

- I haven't worked out in a while, and this is probably going to hurt.
- I have put on some weight and don't want anyone to notice.
- I don't have time to go to the gym.
- If I go to the gym everyone will look at me and judges me.
- I have yet to recover from a previous injury.
- My workout partner is busy.

And the list goes on and on. When you're searching for an excuse to escape the dreaded workout, you typically find it. It is not enough to want to "be" healthy, you must first "do" the things necessary to reach that goal. Action is a key element in a healthy lifestyle. We often fail to take control of our lives, and just let life happen to us. Some circumstances are beyond our control, but how well are we managing the things that are in our control? Being incarcerated is probably one of the most extreme examples of a lack of control. When incarcerated; you are always on other people's time. We try to structure our workouts based upon several different factors. Showers, yard, cellmates, jobs, and passes are just a few. Any change in any of these events can potentially disrupt your plans. Let's take showers for example. A person may choose not to work out because of the absence of an opportunity to take a shower afterwards. If you are a person who does not believe in washing up in the sink, you will undoubtedly find yourself limited when structuring your routine. Those who prefer only to work out in the yard are often also part of the shower chasers. The tricky thing about the yard is that it is prone to cancelation. Weather conditions like lightning and thunder are sure ways to throw a wrench in your plans. The yard is still made available during rain, sleet, hail, or snow, but unless you are one of those all-terrain type of individuals, you might just have to reschedule your workout. Jobs can be an advantage or a disadvantage depending on which one you have. When I used to work in the kitchen, I used to always look for opportunities to get a quick workout in. Especially in the dish room or pots and pans room, one could find small windows of opportunity to do five minutes here or five minutes there. It may not seem like much, but it adds up and the best part about working out while you are at work is that you are guaranteed a shower when you get off. Passes can vary and are not always predictable. If you have a pass (which means you are scheduled to go somewhere at a particular time), unless it is somewhere that you go every week, you may not be notified until the night before. So now you must rethink any work out engagements that you had that were planned around the same time. Yet, the biggest obstacle for many is that of having a cellmate. Regardless of if the two of you get along or not, you still have to be considerate of one another. Nobody's routine will synchronize 100% and it becomes necessary to adjust your routine on the fly. These are just the surface of some of the hurdles we encounter in prison. Many of whom are not familiar with the prison experience think that fitness and prison go hand in hand. The stereotypical prisoner is shredded from head to toe. Even their muscles have muscles. That was what I expected to see upon entering prison but was quickly confronted with reality. Prison is not a army base where people are forced to work out and eat right. It is quite the contrary. It is a place that requires abnormal focus and discipline to avoid being swept up in the foolishness that is so prevalent. It is no different from the streets, in that you have all kinds of people. Fat, skinny, bulky, and ripped alike. I was truly surprised by the lack of motivated individuals. In my mind, we had nothing better to do. This actually was a motivation for many, but it wasn't a sustainable one. As soon as the drugs start to become more abundant, you began to see who was actually dedicated to working out. I watched a many of brothers, several of whom I used to workout with become so taken by drugs, that one could never tell that they were once in an enviable shape. Drugs coupled with the Covid pandemic led many into a downward spiral. During the height of the pandemic, our movement was very restricted. We found ourselves stuck in the cells a lot more than before. They removed all the pull up bars from the yard and denied us access to basketballs. This was a huge blow because some people depend on those things to stay in shape. The worse part of it all was at a time where our movement had slowed down to all but a halt, we started receiving all types of junk food with every meal. Ice cream, muffins, chips, cakes, and cookies were given every day for two and a half years. A blessing during that time was the stimulus money that many of us received. Yet, like with most things, money too can become an object of destruction. The amount of food and drugs being purchased and consumed were at such a high, that supply could seldom keep up with demand. People's appetites and waistlines grew larger and larger, while their discipline grew ever so smaller. As much as we hate to admit it, this microcosm that I live in is but a minor reflection of our greater society. From the dungeon to the hood, to the Hollywood hills, one will realize that the same problems exist.

What my incarceration has taught me is that a made-up mind is a dangerous thing. There's a saying in Jamaica that goes "Take your hand and turn fashion", meaning make do with what you have (and do it well). I don't care who you are or where you are in life, just as easy as it is to find an excuse not to do something, it is equally easy to carve out some space and time to get active. We make time for the things that are important to us. My big brother Ruben and I were having a disagreement one day, because I was sharing my, as he calls it, "just do it" beliefs. He spent half an hour on the phone debating why it is or is not just that easy. He brought up a point that is a go to for many when I am trying to give advice to people who are not incarcerated. The fact that I have been locked up for over a decade and have been in here since I was a child tells people that I just don't understand the woes of ordinary life. Still, I beg to differ. It is true that I am not plagued with some of the difficulties that people in society are confronted with, like having to buy and prepare your own food, paying bills, raising children, going to work and a host of other things.

I cannot argue that I don't have more free time to focus on myself than people on the streets. It would be an insensitive argument to make if I tried. But like I explained to Ruben, my advice is not for the person who is struggling to find their next meal, because in that type of situation, options are scarce. My advice is for people that are living comfortably enough to make healthier lifestyle choices. Ruben argued that sometimes people just don't have the time and are too busy to worry about working out. My question to him was, "are you telling me that people have no time in a day, not even thirty minutes to set aside for their health?" His response was "no, some people don't." His response baffled me, I could not make sense of it. I was trying to figure out how within a twenty-four-hour day could someone not find at least thirty minutes to spare for something as important as their health. That was when the light bulb went on. Neither of us was wrong in our arguments because we were talking about two different things. We were using the same term, but it was lost in translation when I said workout, it conjured a completely different image for him than it did for me. I didn't realize that just that difference in understanding could make the difference in if people could find time to "workout". For me and a lot of people like myself who are or have been incarcerated, have had the opportunity to develop this different understanding of working out than people on the streets. In prison, one learns how to take a more flexible approach to working out, (of course if they are really passionate about it). I have learned to look for even the smallest window of opportunity to do something. I have worked out in the shower, on the tier, in the cell, in the recreation hall, in the yard and of course in the gym. I have been forced to construct workouts that take a maximum of 5 minutes because of certain time restraints. I say all of that to say that I used to assume that people knew to look for the small windows of opportunity and I also assumed that they knew what type of workouts to do within that time frame. I now understand for most people in society, the act of working out is time consuming. The traditional sentiment is that one must travel to the gym, park, or any other exercise destination. Depending on how long it takes to get there, the idea becomes daunting already. Next, we factor in the workout itself. Many people have it in their heads that they have to do something for an hour or more to achieve any type of benefit. We must factor in the workout itself. Many people have it in their heads that they have to do something for an hour or more to receive any type of benefits. Finally, we must factor in the commute home and then your shower. It is safe to assume at bare minimum; this entire process would take no less than two hours. When that is the view of the requirements involved to get a sufficient workout, it is easy to find validity in Ruben's argument. Therefore, I concluded that neither argument is wrong, we were just discussing two different things. I now challenge you to discard the idea that it must be a time-consuming process to consider it exercise. Towards the end of this book, I will include several exercise routines that will specifically benefit the individuals that are extremely pressed for time. It is my opinion that with all the things that threaten our health on a daily basis, we must make exercise second nature. We must make it equal to taking care of our hygiene and feeding ourselves. We should view neglecting physical activity as abnormal behavior. Sometimes it can feel like washing the dishes after you have finished eating. Nobody wants to do it, but the more you let them pile up, the harder it will be later. Exercise is one of those dreaded yet unavoidable things we will encounter in life. Whether we do it or not, one way or the other, we will be affected by it.

Chapter 6

Lifestyle Not a Diet

The message has remained consistent and quite simple throughout this book. We invest far too much time and money searching for miracle cures and quick fixes. The fact of the matter is that we do not invest nearly as much effort into changing our thinking as we do everything else. Is your room actually clean if you throw all the dirty clothes under the bed? What's that smell? It looks good, but something isn't quite right. It is easy to focus on the big visible issues and opt to deal with the others later. The problem with this thinking is that the invisible issues typically cause the visible ones. Without making a concerted effort to fix both set of problems, it will feel like your life is moving in a circle. Like a dog chasing its tail, all your goals appear to be just out of reach. It is great to know why we indulge in certain behavioral patterns, but that is not enough. We must decide if these patterns are in alignment with our lifestyle goals. It is necessary to first think healthy before you can be healthy. One of the most common, yet extreme examples is when people get weight loss surgery without adopting a healthy mindset. Aside from it being a quick fix, it can be dangerous if one does not properly understand and appreciate the process. Weight loss surgery was not designed to be a cure for obesity. It is only meant to serve as a launching pad to your journey. There are various types of weight loss surgeries, but the overall goal is to restrict your intake of food. The stomach is normally reduced in size in order to give you a full sensation after eating a smaller amount of food. People who have this operation done experienced weight loss relatively quickly, because they cannot consume the quantity of food that they once could. The amazing thing about the stomach is its ability to adapt and expand. Therefore, the habit of overeating will eventually stretch their cut stomach to its former size. Once this happens, it is not uncommon to see people gain back all the weight that they had lost and possibly even more than before. The real danger comes in when people resume their bad eating habits immediately after surgery, not allowing their stomachs time to heal properly, causing a rupture which can potentially lead to death. That is exactly why it is so important to be fully committed to whatever it is that you're doing.

Growing up, I watched my mother participate in countless weight loss programs, making me very familiar with the concept of dieting. What I observed from my mother, was that whenever she began a new diet, it made her unhappy. Not the lash out on people kind of unhappiness, but the bright light that she had did not shine as bright. During these programs, I was made aware that she couldn't eat this or that. To me, dieting became synonymous with deprivation. It must have been torture for her taking my brother and me to those fast food places, and only ordering a water for herself.

Most of the diet plans that she started were structured for thirty days or less, and she seldom completed them. For many of us, we fail to realize what impact failure has on our morale. Starting something and not seeing it through may lead you to believe that the goal is unachievable. Most of these diet plans out here promise quick fixes and a set amount of weight loss in a set amount of time. It is impossible to discern what plan was born out of altruism and which was created simply to make money. Nevertheless, we must evaluate the sustainability of these programs. Sustainability is the key ingredient in a healthy lifestyle. You may see a difference on the scale if you have followed the program diligently, but ultimately, once the program is over, you are left to your own devices. It makes sense from an economic standpoint, that a person is made dependent on these programs. The maxim goes, "You give a man a fish, he eats for a day, but you teach a man to fish, he eats for a lifetime". It is not in the financial interest of these programs to "teach you how to fish". They need you to spend your money getting that quick fix and then go gain some weight, so you can come back for another. Our society has had a long-standing tradition of exploiting our vices. For the person who doesn't quite understand the full array of benefits one gets from preparing and cooking their own meals, they become easily enticed by the idea of a quick and convenient meal. The fast-food companies understand this dynamic and take advantage by offering low quality foods at high prices. This lack of discipline and understanding is exploited at all levels and can become overwhelming to those who desire to get their lives in order. The foods we eat should get the same consideration that we would use when purchasing a car. We wouldn't just use any dealer and we would inspect the car as well. I have no doubt that we would make sure we would get the most bang for our buck. When so much money is on the line, it's hard not to be extra cautious when making your selection. Yet little do we realize, we put our lives on the line with careless lifestyle choices. I think it is fair to say that with most of us, we don't know what we are doing when it comes to our nutrition. Most of us play it by ear and by the time we gain some understanding of what's going on, we are usually so deeply invested in our bad habit that it seems almost impossible to consider anything else. Many have made it to their lifestyle crossroads and have yet to commit to a direction. Those who have made it this far and fail to commit are in a unique position. Knowing better and choosing to act on your understanding does not come as easy as it would seem. Old habits die hard, and many are reluctant to venture in a new direction, regardless of the amount of facts that may indicate that there is a better option. The reason for this is our perception. Love is a word that we toss around loosely without careful consideration of its meaning. "I love this, or I love that" we will exclaim. Often, confusing the things that we want with the things that we need. This love that we have for so many things must first be applied to ourselves. Let's explore this concept of self. We exist in two dimensions, our mental and our physical. Neither is separate from the other, yet seldom work together effectively. We are eager to satisfy the desires of our mind without considering the needs of the body. The body is incapable of making strategic decisions without the assistance of the mind. Therefore, allowing your mind to be self-centered and solely focus on itself, ultimately subjects the body to neglect and abuse. To properly love yourself is to continuously seek out ways to care for your body and in turn, protect your mind. A healthy body gives the mind the most support. Where the mind makes the big decisions in the relationship, the body in turn feeds and protects the mind. Leading a healthy lifestyle requires that all choices are made with this understanding. Everything is done for the greater good of one another. With this mindset, it makes it a lot easier to ignore those voices that are calling you to satisfy some craving. The cravings never completely go away but the voices are no longer as loud. It is not necessary that they go completely away either. You now have the ability to decide when to indulge in a particular craving as to not disrupt your routine. This is actually a benefit to your body/mind relationship. In every healthy relationship, compromises are made to the benefit of the whole. Carving out space in your healthy lifestyle for the occasional unhealthy foods makes the whole process realistic. As a former fat kid, I am here to tell you that for me, junk food is here to stay. So, I had to devise a plan that allowed me to treat myself while at the same time honoring my body.

The concept of lifestyle vs. diet is not solely food related. It may also be applied to other areas of life. For many findings order and structure in one's eating habits is probably the most difficult thing to do. You may see some people who are diligent and disciplined in education, job, and Faith, but have chaotic eating habits. I would argue that learning to manage your diet will make managing other areas of your life that much easier. Your nutrition affects your energy level, your stamina, concentration, memory, sight, and countless other aspects of your life. For example, consuming a large amount of sugar or carbs make you instantly tired and unmotivated. Yet an absence of both for an extended period of time have identical effects. Understanding this dynamic makes you wonder why our school systems here in America provides some of the most nonnutritious foods to our children's growing minds. It is not as if the meal planners are unaware of the relationship between nutrition and cognitive ability because the menus are created by nutritionists. The quality of food some students receive may also depend on the school budget. Therefore, when you have such a large disparity of funds allocated to schools, children are deprived equal opportunities to learn. Furthermore, the children in the communities that rely most heavily upon school breakfast and lunch usually belong to the schools with the nonnutritious foods and the small budget. This is just a small example of how fundamental our nutrition is to our overall quality of life. For those like myself who do not have many options to choose from, it is necessary to be hyper vigilant over the choices that we do have.

Conclusion

Putting it all together

We have covered several different topics throughout this book, and none of them are unrelated. The overarching point is that we are a reflection of our thinking and the day-to-day decisions that we make. Every area of our life that is not put under intense scrutiny is subject to disorder. You may have it all together in one particular area of your life and might even be experiencing great success, yet depending on the degree of disorder in other areas will determine to what extent you are able to enjoy your success. We are the architects of our lives, and it is no use complaining about the materials that we have to work with. Once we are given life, it is up to us what we make of it. After spending over a decade in prison, I have had more than enough time to assess my life and the decisions made therein. I believe the most influential moments happen early on in our lives and we carry those experiences with us in one way or another. Often those experiences influence our outlook and effect the decisions we make. A maximum-security prison is a unique environment to be in. At times we experience extreme amounts of isolation which undoubtedly changes an individual. A prisoner is given that rare opportunity to slow down and evaluate their life. Without the throws of everyday life, one is forced to confront themselves. Past, present and future. These extended moments of stillness can make or break an individual. Still, reflecting without seeking the proper solutions may drive you to choose an inappropriate response to your problems. No one has made it to this point in life without a team of advisers and/or influencers. Good, bad or indifferent, these are the people who are nearest to us and help shape our reality. I don't ascribe to the notion that we are all a bunch of individuals simply occupying the same space. Believe it or not, our team consists of people who we both choose and are forced to be around. You know what they say, you cannot choose your family, but we choose the rest of our team based on common interest. It is faulty to analyze ourselves on an individual level. This is not saying don't take responsibility for your actions, but rather, seek to understand to what extent our actions are influenced by others. An example my father always used to give when I was young where "Imagine that your friend says he needs a ride to the store and while you are parked outside waiting on him, he goes in and robs the place" "Guilty by association" he would say. So, what must be concluded from the scenario where you have a friend that puts you in that kind of situation? Is it that he is a bad friend? Remember that you chose him. Instead of wasting time trying to figure out why they are the way they are, try to figure out what purpose they serve in your life. It is hard to end relationships, especially with people closest to you. But if the relationship is leading you in a direction contrary to where you desire to go, then it must be done. You will notice that as you attempt to hold on to some of these dysfunctional relationships, it will become increasingly harder to do. This will be because the two of you are no longer on the same page. My father often says, "two cannot move unless both agree". Therefore, it is imperative that we surround ourselves with likeminded people in order to succeed at developing a healthy lifestyle. I am not suggesting that you cut grandma off because she refuses to stop cooking her fat filled recipes. Some things simply are not going to change. You will continue to live in a world that has health risks at every turn, all the way down to your most intimate spaces. This is why you must find a way to gain control of yourself and the things you do. It can be beneficial to be motivated by something bigger than yourself. It can be God, your loved ones, your career, or whatever else it takes to better hold yourself accountable. When you are surrounded by temptation to revert back to old habits, it can be those people and things that inspire you to stay committed to your lifestyle choices. I speak from experience. Every negative thing that I encountered on the streets was that much more prevalent in prison. On the streets, it was a lot easier to avoid certain obstacles, but in prison, I had to confront many of my old vices head on. When I got locked up, I decided that things like drugs, gangs, alcohol, and other destructive activities did not assist me to become the person I desired to be. Just like with everything, rejection of the behavioral pattern is the first step. But what happens when everywhere around you, you see the people and things with which you were formally associated? It is not as easy as just saying "no." That may work for a person who has yet to be exposed to a thing, but what about those who have already acquired a habit? I remember how I felt when I first came to jail. I felt scared and alone. There were no familiar faces, and I was the youngest amongst everyone. The first time I stepped foot in a jail cell and was finally alone, I looked upon my reflection thinking, "this cannot be my life." I felt completely out of control of my destiny. Right then and there I said to myself, "Ima takes care of you, I promise". The promise I made to myself coupled with a desire to honor God, my ancestors and my elders has been my focal point amongst so many distractions. Those tools gave me the strength to overcome every former bad habit in spite of them being right in front of me. I have had good brothers with what I believe to be good intentions, offer me things that would lead to my destruction. A guy once asked me if I smoked because he heard it was my birthday and wanted to give me a gift. I responded saying "no but I accept books as gifts". You should have seen the look on his face. He looked at me as if I had two heads. The funny thing is, I was dead serious, but needless to say, I didn't receive any books. Two other birthdays, I remember brothers telling me to party with them to celebrate my birthday. One offered me ecstasy and I told him that I was disappointed that he would offer me something that be knew I used to struggle with. More recently, a brother practically begged me to drink although I told him I no longer drink. After he persisted, I asked him "Why do I have to poison myself to celebrate my life." That too gained a puzzled look, but he understood enough to stop asking. I have found that when you decide to conduct yourself contrary to what is considered normal, you may not be met with a warm reception. Choosing to be different, even for the sake of your health is seldom understood. This is where sureness of identity and purpose is most significant. To have an identity is to have definite understanding of who you are, and what you are about. Your identity should never be compromised in order to please others. We tend to have a habit of associating peer pressure solely with young people. Yet people of all ages receive pressure from their peers. Pressure may vary in its intensity and may be benevolent or malicious, but in spite of all of that, it remains the same. It is the tool used to compel someone to do something they would not have done otherwise. We generally hear peer pressure in reference to the young because of their impressionability. The fact that young people are impressionable is only a bad thing when they are targeted by negative influences, yet it is also a gift because they are more open to adopting and developing new behavioral patterns. It is more common to see older people stuck in their ways and less open to suggestions. They usually are the ones who a have defined understanding of who they are. Even if their perception of who they are is a distorted one, it is hard to convince them otherwise. Therefore, understanding that peer pressure is a thing that impacts us all at all ages and more so than others, we should seek out the "good" peer pressure. That's the kind of pressure that motivates and encourages you to do the thing that will add to the quality of your life. If you are unsure how to distinguish between the good and the bad, here are some things to remember. Bad peer pressure normally involves going against your better judgment, sacrificing something, pleasing others, and it typically results in a loss of some kind. Good peer pressure on the other hand will be to your benefit. It will present itself by way of encouraging and supporting you in achieving the positive things that you desire but lack the self-motivation to pursue.

It is rare that you will meet an individual who would not like to improve the quality of his or her life. But, if you by chance run across someone who doesn't, then that means that they either have it all figured out and have reached a ceiling with no room for growth (unlikely) or they have given up striving for better and are content where they are. A lot of times we over complicate things. We put unrealistic expectations on ourselves and set goals that are way beyond our reach. This almost always results in disappointment and depression. It is unfair to yourself if you have spent 30 years eating and living poorly and then expect a 30-day diet and exercise plan to correct it all. "Rome was not built in a day." All great achievements take commitment, persistence, and consistency. The successful people of the world make success look easy. Until you watch a documentary of their journey, you are unable to fully comprehend what it took for them to reach that point. My mother loves to say, "they want my glory but don't know my story." Don't let your measure of success be made using someone else's tools. What the universe has for you was designed specifically for you and must be manifested by you. Far too often we put a dollar amount on success. What we must understand is that money is only an extension of oneself. Virtues like temperance, generosity, zeal, patience, kindness, and humility brings true success to one's life. With those virtues, one often finds the happiness that they were looking for in money.

Prison is such a unique place in that many believe that being released from prison would be the solution to all their problems. There is no doubt that being incarcerated is a depressing situation. These are abnormal circumstances. But if you desire to live a healthy life style, it is imperative that you adopt a positive disposition. Plenty of studies have found that there is a direct connection between mental and physical health. As I am no doctor, I implore you to do the research for yourself. You will find that things like depression and stress have the ability to compromise your immune system. On a less complex level, our thinking directly affects our decision making. When one is sad, depressed, frustrated, stressed, or hopeless even, it is hard for them to execute a plan, let alone make one. I can't begin to count how many times I have heard from the brothers in prison that they are either waiting until they go home to get their life together or at least right before they know they are going home. I have always wondered what the motivation was behind that thought process. To successfully achieve that which you desire, you must have a "just do it mentality". Absent of that, you will always find an excuse available to prolong your progress. If the thought is in your head about what you could, would, or should be doing, then the only question that remains is why not start today instead of some elusive date in the distant future? Sometimes the hardest part when heading in a new direction is taking the first step. Some steps are easier than others and sometimes we prefer to stand still, but the key is to keep looking in the direction that you wish to go. Eventually the feet will follow. I always advise people that no matter what you do, you must give it 100%. Why do you think so many relationships don't work out? Like with everything, without commitment, it is destined to fail. When someone straddles a fence, eventually they will wind up on one side or the other, and when you leave it up to chance; you might not like the side you land on.

Exercises

I never want you to get into the habit of thinking that exercise must be done one way in order to get results. There are a multitude of workout routines out there that can benefit you greatly. I have done almost every exercise that you can imagine (that don't require weights) during my incarceration. Exercising can be a communal process where I have had the benefit of coming across some great teachers and motivators. What I have learned is that many people have the capacity to do the same workouts, but you will notice that a workout routine typically highlights the strengths of the creator. When you begin to take exercise seriously, you will then begin to learn your strengths and weaknesses as well. Although it is important to be self-motivated and not depend on anyone to work out, it may be necessary at times to switch things up and try someone else's routine. Doing this allows you to take yourself out of that comfortability from the familiarity of your own workouts.

People spend thousands of dollars on trainers, and I am not here to complain because they are my colleagues. Having a good trainer can be life changing. They inspire, motivate, and direct you in a way you possibly could not do yourself. Yet far too many people are in need of the same guidance and assistance but lack the means to kick out money for a session. For those who prefer to learn how to fish instead of buying a fish, I would like to share with you some of my secrets. You can spend years studying how the body functions, learning the names of every muscle in the body and how to target a certain area to get a certain result if you want. Most people are deterred by even the thought of that. I have done the heavy lifting for you, so let me give you a simplified version of how it all works. I like to divide exercises into two categories of cardio and strength. Imagine they are both your children, and you desire to treat them equally, never giving one more attention than the other. So, I suggest you spend equal amounts of time performing cardio exercises as you do strength. Cardio exercises can be categorized as exercises that quickly raise the heart rate. Although they may also build muscle, their main function is to increase your heart rate. Cardio exercises like running, jumping jacks, swimming, and bike riding are good example of heart rate raising exercises. It is desirable to raise your heart rate during an exercise because the higher your heart rate, the more calories you burn. Burned calories translates to weight lost. It is very common for people to believe that in order to lose weight in a particular area, one must do exercises specific to that area. You usually find people doing stomach exercises in order to lose weight in their stomach. But it doesn't work that way. Targeting an area of the body fits in the strength category of exercise. When you do exercises like sit ups, it primarily functions to build up the muscle in that area. You may find yourself with the strongest stomach in the world because of all the stomach exercises you do yet cannot seem to figure out why you still have this gut. Aside from poor eating habits that we have discussed in other chapters, failing to choose the proper exercises may prevent us from achieving the fitness goals that we desire. Therefore, if we are looking to see that six pack that we have spent so much time building up, we must employ our cardio exercises in order to burn the fat that conceals it. Then you have strength exercises on the other hand. Any and everything muscle related fits in the strength category. When you do pushups, pull ups, and squats, they all target specific muscles. So, if you desire a firmer butt, leg exercises would assist you in your endeavor. Defining exercise in these two categories of cardio and strength does a great job of simplifying the concept. But there still exists a gray area between the two. The two are never completely separate. You frequently will be strengthening muscles while you are performing cardio exercises and you will experience the effects of a cardio work out while you are doing strength exercises. As I said before, cardio is considered to be exercises that elevate your heart rate. During the course of strength training, if one does not take too long of a break in between sets, you will receive the calorie burning benefit that your increased heart rate will bring. Also, the more muscle mass that you have, the more calories you will burn in general. When designing my work out plan, it is always my goal to create an even blend of cardio and strength so that I can maximize my efforts. Combining the two makes each exercise that much more difficult and more effective. My exercise style can be defined as HIIT (High Intensity Interval Training). It is a series of fast-paced exercises interspersed with slower ones or brief rests. Utilizing this method allows you to keep your heart rate elevated because you are continuously moving. Do not be discouraged by the term "high intensity." It must be understood that what may be intense for one may not be intense for another. People can be on different levels in their exercise journey, but as long as they are raising their heart rate, and strengthening their muscles, the mission is being accomplished. Once you perceive working out from my perspective, it is as if the world becomes your gym. Having an understanding of cardio and strength releases you from the bondage of traditional exercise. Being in prison, for me, It has been an adaptation by force rather than by choice. Prison has brought the creativity out of many. Those incarcerated without access to weights have learned how to make weight bags out of water or books that function as a de facto dumb bell. I have also used toilet paper and socks to function as boxing pads and it is common to see people using their mattress as a punching bag. This goes to show you that the opportunities to get a good workout in is only limited by your imagination. Whenever you see a good flight of steps, it presents an opportunity to run up and down them. A picnic table can be something to jump up and down on and a chair, stool, bench, or ledge can give you something to step up on. These are just small examples of everyday things that we see around us that can be utilized as workout equipment. But, for those who are not the most creative individuals in the world, there is a litany of resources available that provide variety of exercises done in their proper form. No one ever gets all of their routines from one source. As you fix your mind towards fitness, you will begin to learn and adapt workouts to fit your fitness needs. It is ok if you can't do every exercise that you see in a book. Remember the goal is to do something and to have fun doing it. Nothing is more discouraging than pressuring yourself to do something that you might not be ready for. This is a marathon not a sprint, and with commitment, you will be able to fully embrace your new lifestyle.

Eating Strategies

The market for nutritious advice is over saturated and varies drastically. Our understanding on the subject has continued to evolve, as well as both disproving and reaffirming long held beliefs. Within this section, I do not pretend to present a superior strategy. It is my desire to give you a glimpse of what our diets typically consist of on a weekly basis. The following meals are designed by dieticians with the intent to assure that inmates reach their 2,000 calorie daily requirements.

Doc Maryland

BREAKFAST:		**LUNCH:**		**DINNER:**	
Monday					
Applesauce	4 oz	Noodles	4 oz	*Turkey BBQ	[#] 4 oz
Oatmeal W/ Sugar	8 oz	Peanut Butter & Jelly	[#2oz/1oz	Rice	8 oz
Pancakes	3 ea	Carrots	4 oz	Collard Greens	4 oz
Buttered Hot Syrup	2oz	Fruit Cocktail	4 oz	Pudding	1 ea
% Milk	[#]½ pt	Bread/ Goldfish	2sl/1ea	Bread	3 sl
Milk	[#]8 oz	Margarine	1 T		
Tea W/Sugar	8 oz				
**VEG: Griller/Ketchup		[#]3oz/1oz			

Tuesday					
Peaches	4 oz	Hash Brown Potatoes	[#] 4 oz	*BBQ Chicken	[#] 4 oz
Grits W/Sugar	8 oz	Steak Flavored Beef Party	3sl	Mashed Potatoes	8 oz
Scrambled Eggs	[#]4 oz	Corn	4 oz	Mixed Vegetables	4 oz
Bread	3 sl	Fresh Fruit	1 ea	Cookies	2 ea
Margarine	1 T	Mayonnaise	1 T		
Margarine	1 T				

| % Milk | [#]½ pt | Milk | [#8 oz | Tea W/Sugar | 8 oz |
| **VEG: Breakfast Links [#2 ea | | | | **VEG: S1. Veg. Chicken [#] 4 oz | |

Wednesday

Fresh Fruit	1 ea	Oven Fried Potatoes	[#] 4 oz	Chicken Patty	[#] 3 oz
Cocoa Puffs	1 box	*Turkey Bologna	[#]2 oz	Sliced Potatoes	8 oz
Creamed Turkey	[#]4 oz	Cheese	[#]1 sl	Green Beans	4 oz
Bread	3 sl	Tossed Salad/ Dressing	4 oz/1oz	Pudding	4 oz
Margarine	1 T	Fresh Fruit	1 ea	Bread	3 sl
% Milk	[#]½ pt	Bread	3 sl	Margarine/ Ketchup	1 T/1oz
**VEG: Creamed Beef	[#]4 oz	Mayonnaise	1 T	Tea	8 oz
Lemonade	8 oz	**VEG: Okra Patty	[#]3 oz		
				**VEG: Soup/ Bolono	[#]8oz/ 2oz

Thursday

Fresh Fruit	1 ea	Macaroni Salad	4 oz	Roast Beef	[#] 3 oz
Farina/Sugar	8 oz	Pizza	[#]1 sl	Rice	[#] 8 oz
Hard Boiled Eggs	[#]2 ea	Wax Beans	4 oz	Gravy	1 oz
Bread/Pastry	2sl/1 ea	Fresh Fruit	1 ea	Mixed Greens	[#] 4 oz
Margarine	1 T	Fruit Punch	8 oz	Cake	4 oz
% Milk	[#]½ pt	Bread/ Margarine	3sl/1T		
Tea W/Sugar	8 oz				
**VEG: Okra Patty/Ketchup	3oz/1oz				

Friday

Fresh Fruit	1 ea	*Fish Square	[#]4 oz	*Pepper Steak	[#] 3 oz
Rice Cereal W/ Sugar	[#]8 oz	Tartar Sauce	1 oz	Gravy, Ketchup	2oz/1oz
Egg Omelet	[#]4 oz	Spicy Rice	[#]4 oz	Mashed Potatoes	8 oz
Bread/Pastry	2sl/1 ea	Coleslaw	4 oz	Black Eye Peas	4 oz
Margarine	1 T	Fresh Fruit	1 ea	Cookies	2 ea
% Milk	[#]½ pt	Bread	3 sl	Bread/ Margarine	1sl/1T
Cherry Beverage	8 oz	Tea W/ Sugar	8 oz		
				VEG: Egg Salad	[#] 4 oz
**VEG: Crispy Patty/Ketchup	3 oz/1oz				

Saturday

Sliced Apples	4 oz	*Turkey Hot Dogs	[#]2 ea	*Turkey Ala King	[#]6oz
Oatmeal W/ Sugar	8 oz	Baked Beans	4 oz	Buttered Rice	[#]8 oz
Hard Boiled Eggs	[#]2 ea	Sauerkraut	4 oz	Carrots	4 oz
Bread	3 sl	Pears	4 oz	Pudding	[#]4 oz
Margarine	1 T	Bread	3 sl	Bread/ Margarine	3 sl/1T
% Milk	[#]½ pt	Mustard	1 tsp	Tea W/Sugar	8 oz
				Fruit Punch Beverage	8 oz
**VEG: Ala King	[#] 6 oz				
				**VEG: Veg. Burger	[#] 2 ea

Sunday

Plums	4 oz	Kidney Beans	[#]4 oz	*Meatloaf/ Gravy	[#] 4oz/2oz
Grits W/ Sugar	8 oz	**Bean & Cheese Burrito	#1 ea	Mashed Potatoes	8 oz
Waffles	3 ea	Corn	4 oz	Stewed Tomatoes	4 oz
Buttered Hot Syrup	2 oz	Pineapple	4 oz	Cookies	2 ea
% Milk	[#]½ pt	Bread/Chips	2sl/1 ea	Bread	3 sl
				Margarine	1 T
Margarine	1 T				
				**VEG: Soup	8 oz
**VEG: Chicken Roll	[#] 3 oz				

---

*- Meat Containing Foods   **- Vegetarian Alternative

[#] – Potentially Hazardous Foods

The meals provided by this institution looks better on paper than they do in reality. The quality of the food that we receive is substandard. The starches that we most often receive are white and void of any real nutritional value. The majority of the protein comes from a can or a bag, and the vegetables are either also from cans or going bad before they reach the institution. All of this amounts to a well-designed, but poorly executed menu because of the lack of nutrients and the high amounts of sodium.

Yet, all is not lost. Based upon my expertise and personal experience with this menu and others like it, it is capable of providing a steppingstone away from chaotic eating habits and in the direction of a more structured and consistent diet. Those who have access to high quality nutritious foods have an opportunity to use this menu as a template, keeping the structure intact and making substitutions where possible.

A rule of thumb is to look to include carbs, protein, vegetables, and fruit at every meal. Dedicating 45% to carbs, 25% to protein, 15% to vegetables, and 15% to fruit. Portion size will always vary from person to person because everyone does not have the same nutritional requirements, but the divisions should remain the same. There is no one way to create a healthy lifestyle. But when it comes to the things that we consume, we should always seek balance, making sure that we do not omit a particular food group from our diet that may provide essential nutrients.

Acknowledgements

I would like to first Acknowledge God the Most High who has allowed me to wake up every day and strive to be a better version of myself. Next, I would like to pay homage to the Ancestors on whose shoulders I stand (James and Savannah Little) and (Ezekiel and Mary McKenzie) just to name a few. I have been blessed to have a large network of elders that have been my source of Love, Light, Loyalty and Laughter. Mom and Dad (Roy and Belinda McLean), I thank you for never giving up on me and always believing in me. My Aunnie, you have always been like a second mother and one of my biggest motivators to become an author. Aunt Addie, I also thank you for your never wavering love and kindness.

Grandma Hazel, although you have a multitude of kids, grandkids, great-grand kids, and great-great-grand kids, you still make space in your big heart and offer prayers for me and I am not truly grateful to you. Last but definitely not least, Ruben my big brother, you have played a fundamental role in me becoming the man I am today, and I will never stop valuing your opinion. Leroy and Charmaine, my siblings and elders, thank you for always providing me with wise words and taking time out of your busy schedules to talk to me. Big up to my nieces and nephews.

I cannot forget Joshua, Lil Homie, Delmont X, Ragga and many others who have been more like family than friends. Thank you to those I have mentioned and others that I have forgotten for having an impact on me becoming the man I am today.

Printed in the United States
by Baker & Taylor Publisher Services